People Who Moved Me on This Journey

978-0-6151-5769-6

Table of Contents

Dedications
Something about the Author

- The Lott Family
- My Sunday School Teachers
- To All that Showed Love and Support
- To Do Tasks
- Being All You Can Be
- A Christian Life
- Doing What God Tells You
- The Trinity
- I am Proud Of
- How I Could Spend One Million Dollars
- Difficulty About Being A Student
  - Discrimination
  - Who Are You?
  - Being Creative
  - Downtown Las Vegas
    - Come On Out
      - College
      - I Cried
  - Makeesha Britt
  - Andrew Barber
    - Linda barber
      - Caira
      - Kimberly
      - Keylynndra
      - Keylnn Jr.
      - Everything
  - At A Convention
  - Las Vegas, Nevada
    - Going Places
- Children
- To Have Joy
- To Be God
- Obey God
- Sister Martin
- Sister Parham
- Sister Anderson
- First Lady
- Sister Butler
- To The Usher's
- Sister Shirley Scott
- Sister Marshall
- Sister Foster
- Sister Davis
- Sister and Brother Young
- Sister and Brother Mason
- Sister Carmen
- Sister and Brother Bryant
  - Aunt Priscilla
  - Mrs. Kay Lemons
- Mr. and Mrs. Good Dow
  - Calling On Jesus
  - Mother Garrett
  - My Family-NFMBC
  - Family: 01/26/06
- My New Friendship Family
- Happy 34th Anniversary
- Spending Time With Jesus
  - Marriage
- Lessons I Have Learned
- When Things Happen

Copyright © 2007 Kimberly L. Barber-Dorris (West) 978-0-6151-5769-6

My Dedications

To Those That Inspired Me
Special thanks to:

God who is the Head of my life.
My very own family
Doctor Pastor Garrett and Sister Alice
All of New Friendship Missionary Baptist Church
The Barber Family
The West Family
The Dorris Family
The Davis Family
The Malone Family
My Best Friend Makeesha Britt-Clark
Anyone who name was not listed you are not forgotten.

Thank you as well as everyone else that has made a huge impact on seeing me on my way.
Thank you and May God See you through all.
Thanks go to God who has made this all possible.
My heart and love reaches out to everyone that I meet on this journey.

Something about the Author

I was born in Champaign, Illinois on April 18, 1975. I have one brother named Andrew, and one sister who name is Linda Barber. My mom name is Mrs. Mary Lee Barber, who went home in 1992. I have to first give honor to the heavenly Father of my life God's Son Jesus Christ who is the head of my life. I want to thank Him for making this possible for me. God is good all the time. I am glad He changed my life.

I have four children who names are: Caira, Kimberly, Keylynndra, and Keylnn Jr. Who is a joy in my life? I have a wonderful husband named Mr. Mark A. West Sr. I am a member of New Friendship Missionary Baptist Church in Robbins, Illinois since 2005. Before that I was a member of Shiloh Baptist Church in Robbins Illinois. Most of all I am a member of God's army. I also have a good childhood friend who name is Makeesha Britt-Clark who has six children whom are my God children.

Not to leave out I have other Godchildren a shout out too. I am a resident of Robbins, Illinois since 2003 of February. I always enjoyed writing especially as a child and at school. I always wanted to be a writer because I enjoyed it so much that it was my way of talking. Writing is another one of my hobbies; my first is reading the Bible, going to Church, and then writing. Something that come natural for me to do without thinking about what to say.

Thanks for loving me as well.

The Lott Family

I am glad that you all are apart of my life.
I am glad God had you there for me on Tuesday.
I learn from the teaching of the Lord at prayer.
I am happy to know God makes away for all things.
I see the love that you all share with each other.
I feel the warmth of the Lord in what you say.
My heart knows that it comes from the Lord you speak on.
I know that you are children of God's.
I am always ready to learn more from you.
I thank God for you all being in my life.
I thank you for all the teachings at NFMBC.
You encourage me to help others.
Your love sticks with me to share mine.
You are more that just great to know.
I take what you say to the heart.
Everything you teach means something.
I want you to know how much I love you all.

My Sunday school Teachers

Who are apart of my family.
You all have showed me about love in a positive way.
I am privileged to say that I have special teachers.
You all have inspired me to moving more for the Lord.
I see how much the Lord has taught you all.
I am happy to be apart of you all lives and just on Sunday's.
I have learned a lot from you all.
I am thankful to be apart of you all lives at NFMBC.
You all have confident me not to say no to the Lord.
Keep up the good work of the Lord.
I am grateful that you all help me to grow spiritually.
You all have showed me how to keep the Lord near.
I am thankful forth the love we share through Jesus.
I have remarkable time learning.
You all have helped my light from within come out.
I am impressed to do whatever the God asks.
I appreciate what you all teach in class.
I feel the presence of the Lord in you all voices.
I see how far God has brought you from.
I thank God for sending me to your group.
I feel the love that you all reach out to help others learn.

To All That Showed Love and Support

**Thanks to God who made this special event possible.
Thanks to all that prayed for me.
Thanks to all that showed love and support for me.
Thanks for all the back-up and motivation.
This was truly a blessing and know-how.
This meant so much to me.
To all who had my back along the way?
I want to say all the love meant a lot to me.
I was warmed by the love and care.
I know it was the love of the Lord we all share.
Not to say the least-
Thanks again for all the love and kindness.
For the new way of seeing and learning things.**

To Do Tasks

Means to me whatever the Holy Spirit gives.
Such as helping someone turn back to Jesus.
Teaching the Bible to my family.
Having Church at home or wherever I go.
To speak up and out for the rights of others.
To give God His props at all times.
Thanking and speaking about Jesus all day.
Giving the Lord all that He asks of me.
My daily tasks from the Lord.
Praying and listening to the Lord daily.
Time and dedication to the Lord.
Singing and worshiping the Lord.
Feeling the Holy Spirit through my body.
Telling how good the Lord has been to me.
God is always around no matter what the storm is.
Being obedient and willing to do the Lord's will.
Giving up the old life for the new one.
To learn and trust the Lord at all times.

Being all you can be

Is expressing the love of God
Having faith as a mustard seed
Improving from your mistakes
Growing in what God has for me
Justifying what is right
Not letting people run my life
Working on what Jesus has for you to do
Looking to Jesus for guidance
Putting God first, in what you do
Running the race for Jesus
Singing to your heart desire for the Lord
Teaching the fulfillment of Jesus
Understanding God's Word to live by.
Various career options by praying
Being called by Jesus to serve Him.
Calling on Jesus at all times.

A Christian Life

Is all that it can be serving the Lord?
Helps the mind become positive
Opens up a new way to live
A new line of challenges to succeed
Is love for all that accept Jesus
Creates a different environment
A new model person created
Grows you from a infant to a mature person
Gives you a Spiritual connection to God
Plays a tremendous part of your renewed life
Teaches you how to pray
Study the Bible for guidance
You should have a Church home to belong to
Modifies what you need to know
Being able to talk about Jesus everywhere
Loving all God's children as one
Put the old life to rest
Take on the new one
Growing as a Christian is healthy for the soul

Doing what God Tells You

Putting Him on the top of the list
Asking Him for advice
Telling people about Him
Turning all over to Him
Waiting on Him when trouble comes
Dancing when He says dance
Joy all the days of your life
Goodness that He provides
Helping someone who can not see
Reaching out to someone you never seen
Loving someone who is hard to love
Reading the Bible daily
Doing what the Word says
Letting the Holy Spirit in
Praying for someone regardless of who it is
Keeping the Faith in Him at all times
Spending time talking to Him in private

The Trinity
God the Father, God the Son,
and God the Holy Spirit

Joyful is He
Everlasting Father
Superior above all
Upholding what He says
Sensible in all His ways
-
Generous with all He created
Outstanding love He shared
Devoted to saving all His children
-
Happiness that He has for us
Organized the twelve apostles
Loyal to all that serve Him
Young in Spirit
Super in His teachings
Powerful with His words
Impressive in His miracles
Reliable no matter what the situation may turn
Incredible in all His ways
Tender at heart for Him in all our lives

I Am Proud Of

The Creator
God for loving me.
God for changing my life.
God for His love.
Blessings
My children
Stuffy
His Word
His teachings
God for who He is
God's animals
God's family
Grace and mercy
Where I am Today
Being able to be myself
Writing from the heart
Speaking to those about Jesus
My NFMBC family
All of God's children
Those who believed in me.

How I Could Spend One Million Dollars

By giving God His for blessing me with it.
I would fix my home with the needed repairs.
I would pay off all my debts.
I would put away for my children future.
I would build a place for the homeless in Robbins.
I would have a place for children to come and relax.
I would have Gospel Jams for the community.
I would help educate those that are struggling through.
I would help those come to Jesus for themselves
I would rebuild the community in Robbins.
I would offer a place for those that need meals, clothes, and shelter.
I would give out school supplies to all the children.
I would help my fellow Christian brothers and sisters.
I would open a place for people in Robbins to shop

Difficult about Being a Student

Assignments
Changing classes
Lectures
The work
Catching the bus
Being a new student
Getting stranded
Looking for your classes
Late work
Pop quizzes
Making up assignments
Tests
Being late
No breaks
Long hallways
No homework
Summer breaks
No activities
Many different sections

Discrimination

A prejudice against a person,
place or thing.
People skin color
God
Sex
Different races
Cultures
Television
Food
Clothes
People
Things
Homes
Transportation
Higher power
Love
Hate
Happiness
Places people go
Who they hang out with
Where you go
Churches
Be a leader not a follower

Who Are You

You are...

God's children
Special
Unique
Different
Beautiful
Handsome
Wonderful
Talented
Skillful
Excellent
Happy
Loved
Original
Gracious
Precious
Thankful
Terrific
One of a kind
A neighbor
A friend

Being Creative

Being led to the Lord
Learning who you are
Doing what God gave you
Writing unique
Many new skills
Spiritual growth
Joining a loving Church family
New and exciting talents
Opening up a new world
Being able to express your joy
Letting your light shine bright
Reaching out to another
Showing someone else to Jesus
Giving what the Lord says
Talking about the goodness of
the Lord
Living the life God gave you
Walking the path of newness
Loving all people at anytime
Knowing that we are all God's
children
Standing through the tests that
you are given
Never giving up or looking down

Downtown Las Vegas

A beautiful place to visit.
Many spots to go gambling at.
Different places to go see.
A movie screen shaped like a dome.
Many big flat screen televisions on buildings.
Some television along the long walkways.
Oh! How hot it gets there.
Some hotels sprinkle water when it is hot.
Many large water fountains everywhere.
Many mountaintops to be seen all over.
An old fashion train used as a restaurant.
New buildings are being built.
Tall funny shaped hotels created.
Some long, large hotels and small ones too.
Escalators are all over the place you go.
Families are vacationing a lot.
Some people laughing at things they say.
Music is playing everywhere you go.
Casino's cling-clinging as you go by.
The food smells so good makes you want some.

Come On Out

At times, when the world is just
plain dark all around.
When children want to fight
your all the time.
When you need directions from
someone.
At times, when problems bring
you down.
To hearing an inspiring message
of faith-hope-and love.
When confusion and arrogant
people stare at you.
At times, when you do not see
away through yourself.
Where parents do not want to
teach there child/children about
God.
When times are carried away
and you try to solve it.
When you reach out to someone
for him/her to hurt you.
When you want to go to another
level in your life.
Where things around you are
pulling at you.
At times, when you do not think
you are going anywhere.
To find how Jesus can change
your world around.
Words of encouragement that
will help you on the way.
To be filled with what God has
given you to live.

College

Can take you as long as you like.
Is another life after high school?
Teaches many different courses.
Have wonderful teachers and classes.
Can take you anywhere you want to go.
Has small to large classes to choose from.
Counselors and Advisors to help with whatever.
You have a choice to choose what you want to do.
Have some large areas to sit in and use the computers.
Many stairs to climb or the use of the elevator.
Funds are available to help with schooling.
Scholarships are available to those that qualify.
Tutoring and other things that can be of use to you.
A schedule that is suitable to your own needs.
What is best and will work for you.
Can be attended on to seven days a week.
Touches in a splendid way.
Grows educationally to you on another level.
Has a degree or certificate program.
A place many people want to go but do not have a chance.

I Cried

When I was born
As a child
Anytime I got hurt
All the time as a kid
At everything
Being by myself
Some time's to sleep
When I was very blind
Whenever my feelings were hurt
Watching television
Playing games with my family
Learning to ride a bike at
thirteen
Walking to school
In any type mood
Any place or time
When someone say something to
me
My love for the Lord
Being changed
Happy situations
Graduating high school

Makeesha Britt (Clark)

My hometown best friend.
Who enjoys music?
Has a wonder art talent.
Excellent as a friend.
Elegant in all she does.
Sings with grace.
Has a good humor.
Always alert and ready.
Goes overboard to help someone.
Will do what is asked of her to do.
Loves her family and friends.
Has had my back along the way.
She stretches out her love.
Mature as she can be.
Alert as she can to help.
Kind no matter who is around.
Excellent in all she says.
Extreme to the max as a friend.
Humorous to making you laugh.
Sings within her heart with love.
Artistic as she draws what she feels.

My Brother
Andrew Barber a.k.a AB

My loving brother
To one I love dearly.
One active brother.
Who carries himself neatly?
Always working hard.
Nice to be around.
Does what it takes to moving up
Radical in conversations.
Excellent in caring for others.
Wonderful to be around.
I am glad to have you as a brother.
Whom I love with all my heart.
Happy to know you are alright.
I am thankful to see you.
Pleased to talk with you in person.
We have shared some hard times together.
Growing strong in your responsibilities.
On the go for what you want in life.

Linda Barber

My blood sister who birthday is December 29.
Who lives in Champaign, Illinois with her mom?
An incredible child of God's.
Has a love different than others.
Has her own way of doing things.
Who I would like to know better.
Got separated from me as a child.
Stuff happened that confused me.
I have tried to do my best to be there for you.
I have written letters and cards to you and nothing in response.
No matter what happens I am always going to be your sister.
I have a big love for you that you do not understand about me.
You are a precious in my life even if you do not feel the same way.
Nothing can replace you in my life.
I remember all the visits and fun times we shared as children.
All the fun times we all three shared together.
You are a lovely lady.
You are intelligent.
You are nice to be around.
You are delightful to talk to.
You are alert about a lot of things.
Do not old on to the past, let it go.
Trust Jesus in your life.
He will help you through anything that is troubling you.
I am always going to be on your side with much love.
Whenever you are ready to be apart of my life for real.
I love you more than you can think.
I miss you.

I am happy to be your mom.

Caira

You are a bright loving child.
You are one of God's gifts.
You are fun to be around.
One who loves to sing and usher at church.
She loves her family who is close at her side.
Who has lots of sisters and brothers?
Is twelve years old at the time?
In addition is in the seventh grade.
For fun likes to read, study, and play games.
There are many foods that she enjoys eating.
Very active at the community Center in Robbins.
There are many things that she wants to accomplish.
You are very charming young lady.
Enjoys life to the fullest that she can.
Has a wonderful smile that can not be resisted.
Shows affection to many who knows her.
As precious as a gem held in your hand.
Appreciates her Church family.
Fun and sweet to be around.
Open to learning new things with help.

Kimberly E.

My second precious gift from God.
She is eleven years old at the time.
Enjoys basketball, art, music, and her family.
Likes to read, sing, draw, and learn things.
Is an Usher and choir singer at Church.
She is in the sixth grade at Nathan Hale Middle School.
Her family and the Lord is her guide.
She loves her family at New Friendship in Robbins.
She talks about God and many more things of interest.
She has fun being with her family.
An interesting young girl who knows what she wants.
Playful and amusing to be around.
A precious diamond to have.
Fun and enchanting as a child.
Very happy and full of life.
At times do not want to be bothered.
I am pleased to be able to be your mom.

Keylynndra

My third blessing from the Lord above.
Is most friendly to love but shy at times.
She loves her family that helps her on her way.
She is happy to attend functions at Church.
She is active in the Community Center and an Usher.
She loves to sing, dance, draw, and have fun.
He enjoys attending New Friendship MB Church.
He has great fun doing what interest her.
She is very cute to be charming as a teddy bear.
She knows what things she likes to do for fun.
Has the means to do whatever one asks her to do.
Take fun into going out to restaurants.
She is in the fifth grade at NHI.
In her free time, she likes the library.
She likes to learn about Jesus at home and Church.
Most of the time she attends Sunday school.
She just makes you want to love her all the time.
A very cozy heart that one wants to love.
Playful who is talkative at home?
Is most gracious to love and know in my life.
I am proud to be her mom.

Keylnn Jr.

My son from the Lord.
Is full of love and energy to share.
He is very playful and often misunderstood.
He enjoys singing, dancing, and playing.
Loves Church and singing to everything.
Enjoys his family and Church members.
Attends the Community Center in Robbins.
In addition attends Nathan Hale Primary School.
He is also in the second grade.
He likes to be the baby boy in the family.
Likes to be the center of attention at the party.
Fun to be around no matter what he does.
Does what he is asked most of the time.
He is a joy to who I love.
Likes to get on his sister nerves, sometimes.
Is very helpful most of the time.
Will listen to directions most of the time.
He is whom I am proud of in my life.
I am thankful to be his mom.

Everything

That is God my all and all.
The sun which shines bright.
The rain that pours down.
The clouds when shaping.
My family who I love greatly.
The mountains that move out.
Lightning that strikes many places.
Thunder that rolls over us.
The Earth the revolves around.
The moon that has many faces.
The water that we use.
High places that we have feared.
Low places that has changed our lives.
Tests that approach our lives.
The stars that are in the sky.
Jesus being the Son of God.
Snow that can be shaped.
Wind blowing all the time.
People who we want to teach about Jesus.
The love which is in order to spread out.

At a Convention

A huge gathering among many people.
People from all over the world attend.
Many lectures and information gathered.
Poetry is being read out loud too many.
All types and styles being heard.
A variety of age groups are there.
A meeting of famous poets there to talk.
A performance by Tony Orlando.
A song by Reuben Stoddard.
Five famous Poets performed.
At one of the largest hotels, the Rivera.
People selling there merchandise.
Lots of long lines to wait in.
Books to be given out for autographs.
Being able to register for a spot.
Certain types of Christians are there.
One of these is hosted every year to Poets.
A great experience for one to have in there life.

Las Vegas, Nevada

A city way bigger than the city.
Many places to go and see.
A lot of different Casino's.
Tons of hotels and motels.
More places than I ever seen.
Some two level buses called "The Deuce."
Buses that turn when it moves.
A train that goes in the air.
Many places that are fun to go to.
Different shows of performances to watch.
Buses running every 5 to 20 minutes.
Some run all night long there.
Many mountain tops to be seen.
Places to walk to and from.
Quiet places to relax at.
A great adventure and getaway.
I have enjoyed the monorail bus.
Walking around Downtown and along the Strip.
Farms and fun worlds to play at.
Creative buildings being out up around town.
Many sites to go around and see.

Going Places

Can mean so many things to us.
Is doing something that you
want to do.
Means climbing higher and
higher not on drugs.
Does one good on the inside to
the out.
Helps one know what they can
accomplish in life.
Shows you where you can go
when you try.
Takes place in many people lives.
Has meaning to different spots in
life.
Teaches many things than God
created.
Gives ideas of places to go to and
see.
A since of being yourself for you.
Something that you want o know
more about.
Places that will capture your
attention.
Going out and exploring new
sights to visit.
Doing what you want to do for a
chance to grow.
Taking your family out with you
sometimes.
Adventuring what you can do
instead of not trying.
Taking out the old things that
way you down.
Reaching higher mountains that
you want in life.
A show of maturing to the next
point of this walk.

Children

Are most precious to be around with joy.
Children are told they wish they never existed.
Some children are very amazing to see.
Children are a grand gift from God to love.
Some you do not want to be around.
Children have a way of reaching out to some.
Most children are looking for love.
Some children are fun to love.
Time to time we are all children at heart.
Children are a great gift from God.
They should only be loved and cared for.
Children are precious as jewels.
They require special attention by all.
Some children do not know love.
Children are who we once were.
They are all different and special to all.
Some children are disrespectful.
People often abuse there children.
Children are often abandoned by there mom.
Some are burned in fires.
Children are often molested.
Some are tossed out like trash.
Children are often cursed at.
Some of them are special needs.
Children are neglected daily.
Without children then we would not be here.

To Have Joy

To have joy is a blessing from God.
When the Lord wakes you another day.
Is in the noonday
In the evening
At bedtime
Studying the Word
Going to school
Having Church anywhere.
Listening to God speak
A peaceful day
Time with your family
The Spirit down on the inside
Watching your children get on the bus.
Singing unto the Lord from within.
Love
Can be spread to someone
Everything created
Is to have hope
Spreads what Jesus has done for you.
Does one good on the inside and outside.
Helping someone come to Jesus for themselves.

To Be God

My Protector who keeps me safe
A Friend who is there when I need Him.
My Leader to stir me the right way to go.
A Healer when I am in pain or hurting.
A Savior to teach me what I need to know.
My Teacher to teach me things along the way up.
My Comforter when no one is available.
A Helper to motivate me through all things.
My Guider for when I was very lost.
A shoulder to cry on at anytime I want.
My Doctor for if something needs to be looked at.
A Blessing who has carried me up and out of tests.
A lover of mine that knows me for me only.
My family to do things with everyday given.
A Miracle that died on the cross for our sins.
My Homey to kick it with as I want to daily.
A Source whom I can count on all the time.
An educator to teach His knowledge to us.
A tester to see if we can make it to the next level.

Obey God

This means to all of us...

His Word
The Love
The Temple
Our Body
His House
The Faith
His Love
The Hope
The Trinity
All His children
The Bible
All Preachers'
His Will
The Members
His Family
The Plants
All Animals
The Food
People in Authority
The Workers of His
Every Christian
Many Sacrifices
Even those who cross you wrong

Sister and Brother Martin

To the wonderful Martin's, I have grown to.
Sister Martin is a magnificent woman of God.
Brother Martin is a unique man of God.
The Prayer Band leader, who teaches about prayer.
My sister and brother who I am happy to be near.
They are excellent teachers.
I enjoy what they teach.
Is always on the move for the work of Jesus.
They are special friends and family in my life.
They have the heart of God all over them.
Share what the Lord has done for them.
Loves there precious family as much as possible.
Raised God-fearing children who love the Lord.
They share a wonderful bond on a personal level.
Speaks of what she has been brought from in her life.
Has influenced many people in their lives.
A smile that warms many hearts regularly.
Stays in the Word of God everyday.
Is willing to be ready when the Lord calls them.
They both of full of God's Word and Spirit daily.
They are exceptional to me on this walk for Jesus.
I am glad that I have got to know them for myself.

Sister Diane Parham

To my special friend and sister who I love.
I like the way you take time to teach the young.
The way you take time to speak individual with.
I know that you are true to what you do for Jesus.
I thank you for loving me just for me.
You are wonderful and give great hugs.
You inspire me to stay with the Lord in my life.
You help teach me things I do not know.
I am very comfortable being around you anytime.
When I see you, I know that I can be near you.
I am happy that you help all the children sing.
Being around you I learn a lot from overtime.
I enjoy all the talks and laughs we share.
Knowing you for myself is a warming feeling.
You are a great director to both choirs.
I can feel the Spirit when I am near you.
I know that you do everything in love of Jesus.
In the raw your love is widely spread throughout.
I hold on to the inspirations and knowledge gave.
Thanks for your love and patience that you have.
Thanks for being a big part of my life as well as my family.

Sister and Brother Anderson

Two very gracious people I am glad to know.
A special friend who is in my heart always.
Who takes the time to teach us to sing for Jesus?
Has cheering words of knowledge to say.
Has a big love like Jesus does.
Who feels the Spirit of the Lord in their life?
Knows her members on a personal level.
They have a smile that draws on into them.
Are a marvelous teacher and instructor of the choir?
They have a way of serving the Lord to follow.
Is true in praising the Lord as their Savior.
Who teaches others what they know about Jesus.
Has a fantastic singing voice from the Lord.
Is firm for what they do for the Lord?
Very understanding for the Lord in their lives.
I am delighted God put you all into my life.
Thanks for giving me a chance to sing for Jesus.
To whom I love forever and always.
This is my show of appreciation to you.
You are very magnificent inside and out.
I am glad that I am around you when I am.

First Lady
-Alice Garrett

I just want you to know how I love you.
You are my sister as well as a friend in my life.
I gain knowledge from what you say to me.
I see how wonderful you are on the inside and out.
The way you walk for the Lord in your life.
You are a precious wife to your husband.
I remember all the great things you say to me.
You are warm and very loving to me and others.
I see how much God is in your life.
You have the voice of an angel when you sing.
I feel the sincere warmth from your words.
Your love is bigger than any ocean.
You are so wonderful and happy all the time.
I think that you are an amazing woman of God.
Love able in all your ways of the Lord shared.
In your obedience you are well loved to the max.
I see an intelligent uplifting woman with love.
Is very courteous when doing work of Jesus.
Has an encouragement for all God's children.
When the Lord created you, He made an Angel.
You are such a generous and outstanding person.
Thanks for teaching and loving me as one of your own.

Sister Butler

An excellent Sunday school
Teacher to have,
To whom God has filled to be in
my life.
Has the patience to teach others
about Jesus.
Is most friendly and smiling all
the time.
Has a big faith in the Lord
always.
Loves the Lord from her heart
out.
My glorious sister as well as a
friend.
Also a member of the Senior
Choir.
Is very joyful in the Spirit of
Jesus.
When I see you I am glad to be
near you.
To have such a fine conversation
and big hugs from.
Sings so delicately to the Lord all
the time.
The love that continue to inspire
me each day.
A hope that warms me when I
see you.
Is a strong motivated woman of
God?
Is moving for the Lord's will to
be done.
Has God written all over
everything that you say?
A great shiny part of my family
as we grow.
I am happy to be in your class
and learn all I can.
You are a fine and loving person
whom I am proud of.

To the Usher's

Doing the work that you do is not an easy one.
Seeing how wonderful you all greet people.
The love that you all have for everyone.
Being able to shake and hug someone is love.
You all take time to mold the Junior Usher's.
Showing them the way is being appreciated.
Being dedicated to serving for the Lord is good.
Going out of your way to make sure things are in order.
Taking the time to share what you all know.
Speaking to everyone on a personal level.
Helping the Junior Usher's to practice class.
To be able to help others find a place to sit at.
The way you walk the Pastor to his seat.
The walk that you walk for Jesus in your lives.
The encouragement that you do a swell job.
You have a way of doing what the Lord gives you.
For the wonderful greetings and welcomes you say.
The love and smiles that fill any room any place.
Being delightful in things that move to Jesus.
You are not just an Usher but my family too.
You all do a splendid and marvelous task.

Sister Shirley Scott

Is a very pleasant person to have as a friend?
Who inspires me to keep on moving for the Lord?
Has spent different times with me one on one.
Who I have fun being around at anytime.
Very encouraging and uplifting always.
Has a noble sense of humor that makes you laugh.
Someone that I can talk to not just as a sister.
An exceptional woman who loves Jesus.
When she loves you she really loves.
A reliable woman who is distinctive in my life.
An encourager too many people that she meets.
Has a talented singing voice used for the Lord.
Has a way of showing God's love for everyone.
Is ready for an assignment from the Lord.
On the move from the Lord when He calls her.
Is the same no matter when you see her?
Wants the best for all God's children.
Makes sure you are on the right page in life.
Is always high in the Spirit all the time.
Enjoys life to the fullest that the Lord gives.

Sister and Brother Marshall

The Prayer Band Leader at New Friendship.
Is loved by my heart and me.
Not enough words to express there love.
Shows you how to pray to the Lord.
Teaches what can be absorbed through Jesus.
Has an exclusive approach of teaching the Word.
Does great things that the Lord gives to them.
Hugs that are filled with the warm touch.
Love that can be captured and held on to.
Talks with the Lord on this journey daily.
Speaks in such a fashion that you love to here.
A handshake that just moves you right in.
An encouraging word of thought to remember.
Knows how the Lord has touched there lives.
Takes the time to say what the Lord has done.
Grooves for the Lord and His work being done.
Has touched the hearts of many with love.
A growing touch that only you can know from them.

Sister Foster

One of my teachers in Sunday school.
Has a great smile to share with many.
Loves to teach about Jesus to all.
Loves her family as much as can be.
Takes the love given out to others,
Speaks with words that can be felt.
Opens her arms to all God's children.
Has a wonderful way of showing love.
A hug that makes one feels brand new.
Sings in a unique way that can be touched.
Loves that love of the Lord everyday.
Helps others to understand about Jesus.
Knows how to reach others coming to Jesus.
Is precious in every way that brightens the day.
Most special in my heart which I love.
Does what the Lord gives for her to teach others.
Talks in a polite manner with tons of love.
Will help you to grow into the Lord for yourself.

Sister Regina Davis

A great woman of God.
Has a bright smile one can see.
Teaches with love that you would like to feel.
Full of sincere hugs when she is around.
Has a special love for all people.
Talks in an authentic way to all people.
Is a nurse with many wonderful ways?
There when people need her to do something.
Knows the Lord in a way that helps her through.
Does helpful tasks given from the Lord.
Enjoys what the Lord does in her life.
Loves her family in a loving way to feel.
Is very motivating to share kind words with.
Makes one feel outstanding when near them.
Touches in a striking way of the Lord.
Walks in the way that she teaches to others.
A presence that can be felt as you know her.
Loves all children that she touches in an amusing technique.

Sister and Brother Young

A brother and sister to me.
Are my buddy and helper to learn from?
Apart of God family to love exclusively.
A heroic father to his children.
Has been good to my family in growth.
Are good quality people who I am proud of?
Speaks highly about Jesus to all.
Complete at stimulating people of the Lord.
Has a lot of knowledge about the Lord.
Apart of my family and heart as well.
Who I gain education from through conversation.
Does things with only being asked once.
Have the love of God within and out.
A smile that light a room full of people.
Treasured in my book and heart.
Treat every person kind as they can be.
I am thankful to have them in my life.
Teaches the girls to be proper Usher's.
The love that they have for each other is special.
The line of communication with them is rare in every way.

Sister and Brother Mason

Very wonderful Christians.
A magnificent family to love.
Exclusive in the Lord's eye.
Are extraordinary to my family.
Cheering for Jesus with love.
Many harmless conversations given.
Fantastic hugs that are felt.
Constantly happy in the Spirit all day.
A peace only Christians know.
Help at anytime when needed.
Does what the Lord gives from the heart.
Never says anything that is bad only good.
Is very loving in every way.
Gives love at all times of the day.
Has a positive word to say always.
A smile that will touch your soul.
In high spirits as the sun shinning.
Goes a mile or more for the Lord.
Thanks for being apart of my family.

Sister Carmen Rhodes

Another special person in my life.
One of God's children who I love from my heart.
Who has a lot of encouragement to give out?
Teaches the children about Jesus at Sunday school.
Enjoys what the Lord pouts on her heart.
Takes time to teach those who are lost be found.
Helps souls to reach Jesus for themselves.
Goes out of her way for all people she meets.
Helps you to understand more about Jesus.
Spends time reading good Christian books.
Helps out with many projects at Church.
Knows how to love like no one else.
Has a wonderful time getting to know others.
Is full of the Lord's power within herself.
Builds out to reaching all through the Lord.
Stays content while teaching about Jesus.
Has a unique way of loving others fully.
Someone that I take an ear to grow with.
A mighty sister in Jesus Christ to love always.
I am glad that God has sent her into our lives.
A great smile that you can feel from a mile away.

Sister and Brother Bryant

My family and friends.
I am glad that God has put you
in my family.
I enjoy the encouraging words.
I am thankful to know you.
You have great motivation skills.
Listening to you preach, is
pleasing.
The way you share God's love.
The special love you have for
God.
Being encouraged by the Lord.
Stay moved by the Lord for all
things.
You are always the same no
matter what.
The way you take time for others
Letting God use you to do His
work.
A positive understanding for
others.
For being grateful for all things.
Being obedient in what the Lord
says.
An outstanding job with open
arms.
You are wonderful parents.
People who love the Lord at all
times.
Happy to tell others about Jesus.
A grand way of helping other
people.

Aunt Priscilla Dyson

You are most loved and appreciated.
I am pleased to be your niece.
You are a great Aunt to have.
I know a satisfied woman of God.
I see a brilliant mother of four children.
You are an inspiration to many people.
I feel the love we share that God gives.
You are very precious as a rose full bloomed.
You gave time to know me as your niece.
I am fortunate that God put me in your family.
You are sweeter than the honey from a tree.
Your love moves my heart.
I benefit from the warm conversations that we shared.
Your wonderful hugs brighten the day.
I believe the presence of peace you have.
I appreciate that you are a strong person.
When God created you, He smiled pleasing.
I am grateful for the times we shared.
I understand a favorable married woman who loves her family.

Mrs. Kay Lemons

My angel who helped me through high school and after.
Who was always there when I needed someone?
Helped me find my way when I could not see.
Often took me to church with her family.
Has done things for my family along the way.
Encouraged me to graduate high school.
Selected me to win the Central Pride Award.
At times let me come to her house.
Was one that made an impact on my life?
There when I came to school early.
Would give me a ride home after school.
All of my children God Mother.
Was there when I had my first child.
Believed in me when no one else did.
One who I will always remember and love dearly.
Shared her family with me and taught me things.
Spent time with me when no one else would.
Drew me close to her heart and kept it there.
Seen me through prom all the way.

Mr. and Mrs. Good Dow

Two very special people of God.
Has the love of God all over.
Is precious to be around.
Helpful whenever you can.
When I see them, I just love them.
They are very sweet to know.
They are swelling to be around.
They do what God tells them to.
They are good gifts of God.
I am privileged to see and speak to them.
They have realness in the Lord that takes you.
They have a great family to be in the mist of.
People who shows love and concern.
A family to be apart of through God.
A love that makes a million smiles.
A conversation that touches the heart.
A family that I am pleased with.

Calling on Jesus

When you wake-up every morning.
When you are praying.
When good things happen.
When bad things happen.
When your neighbor's are rude.
When you have tests going on.
When you have the Spirit on the onside.
When you need a shoulder to lean on.
When people come against you.
When you breathe fresh air.
When you can see the sun shinning.
When you have unpleasant days.
When you want to go off the deep end.
When your children goes to school.
When your bills are due.
When you need some answers.
When you need guidance.
When you are happy.
When you get sad sometimes.
When you want a better way.
When you need someone to talk too.

Mother Garrett

Dr. Pastor Garrett's mom and Mother of the Church.
A precious and angelic woman.
Someone special and unique.
A genuine and sweet woman of God.
A mighty mature and loving woman who raised fine children.
The love of God in everything you say and do.
How kind and humble you are to the Lord.
A proud black woman whom I admire to the fullest.
Your heart is bigger than any mountain.
Your smiles more than a million words.
The family closeness that makes my heart grows.
The warmth that I feel when I shake or hug you that makes me knows love.
I know it is good when I see you every week.
Whenever I speak with you I feel peace and joy.
I enjoy how much God has taken you in life.
Being around you and knowing you are a great person.
Your love is greater than any rainbow.
Your life has really made an impact on me.
I look up to you.
You are very dedicated to your family and friends.
I am glad to say and be apart of this family through Jesus Christ.
I am able to see how much faith and love you have for everyone.
I am pleased that God has blessed you to be in my life.
I am thankful for being apart of the New Friendship Family.
To know that your children are very respectful, loving, and Christian.
I am glad to say, "Mother Garrett, You are apart of my life and I Love you!"

My Family
-NFMBC

To those who God has put in my life on the way.
To all of God's children.
I want to show my appreciation to God.
To those that helped me on the way.
For those that have allowed me to be apart of their lives.
To God for putting me in you all lives.
For helping me to grow stronger in the Lord.
For the encouragements from the Lord.
All the sermons and lessons being taught.
For the patience with my children.
The love and warmth that we all share.
To take time to teaching me God's wisdom.
The Bible Study lessons that I come to learn from.
Being apart of the prayer meetings at Church weekly.
For being special in my growth of Jesus Christ.
Spiritual growth in Christianity.
The life messages to grow on in my life.
To reaching out to learn what God said?
I am grateful to God on my mission and love.
Thanks!

Family: 01-26-06

When I think of family, I think about the West Family.
Being apart of the West Family is a new and improved part of my life.
First I want thank the Heavenly Father who is God.
Thanks for putting me in the West Family.
The West Family is a blessed family to be in.
The West Family has taught me a whole lot about what real family is.
Sine I was accepted into the West Family, I have experienced new things.
The West Family is a very special part of my life and my children.
To my family may we have a togetherness to share with all?
The West Family is more than just family.
To my family we shall stand strong in the Lord and as a whole unit.
The West Family has taken me on a completely new journey.
To my family we want you to continue to be apart of our lives.
The West Family is where I am glad that the Lord moved me too.
To my family we want to extend our love and hearts to all members.
The West Family has helped me to appreciate the meaning of family.
To my family may God continue to bless you and grow us closer together?
The West Family has opened my heart and mind to people.
I am grateful for all that the Lord is doing in my life.
The West Family has showed me a new beginning.
I am grateful and thankful to the Lord for all that He has done.
The West Family is why I have grown in love, and God's teachings.
To my family we are thankful to all that have helped me along the way.
We are glad to be in a loving family.
The love that we have for one another.
The many family reunions that our family have together.
All the gatherings that brings memories.
Having family fun that brings everyone together.
The quality time that we have for one another.
Peace and Joy that comes naturally.
The love of God that are in all of us.

My New Friendship Family

What they mean to me on this
journey from the Lord.
Most of all, I thank God for
leading me to such a wonderful
place.
They have helped me
tremendously and spiritually
grow.
They have helped me climb the
ladder to great places.
They have shown me love at a
new perspective.
They love me for what God sees
in me.
They are encouraging and
uplifting.
They are very special and unique
to my family.
They have motivated me to
reaching out.
They are teaching me the way of
the Lord.
They help me to sing out to the
Lord from within.
This to me is what a real church
family is all about.
They take the time to help me
seek the Lord for all things.
They have taught me to spend
time with the Lord one on one.
They taught me to pray, sing,
help, and obey the Lord.
They each have a special place in
my heart.
I have learned a lot from each
and everyone that are there.
How they take time for my
children to learn?
When they talk with us on a
special level of growth.
When the many doors have
opened since, I have been there.
Every step of growth comes from
the Lord, and all who want their
lives to change.
Without you all me and my
family now know what being
saved is all about.
I just want to extend my thanks
and gratefulness to everyone.
I am on a whole new page and
you all helped me revive to A
New Way to go.

Happy 34th Anniversary

Pastor Dr. Garrett

To the greatest Pastor in the world, who God has made.
To the child of God who has inspired me.
To the one who also believes in me?
The one that has helped my family on the way.
To the one that speaks what the Spirit gives him.
To the one that teaches what the Bible says.
To the one that has a big heart.
To the one that has costiveness when he speaks.
To the one that has made it another year preaching the Word.
To the one that encourages each and every member of the family.
To the one that holds what the Heavenly Father tells.
To the one that expresses long life in his teachings.
To the one that is unique and special in everyday.
To the one that was put in my family life.
To the one that gives spectacular messages of love, weekly.
To the one that is very obedient to the Lord.
To the one that is truthful and honest, no matter what.
To the one that is loved by many people along the way.
To the one that have touched the lives of many, many people.
To the one that has a place in my family and heart.
To the one that I love for being God sent in my life.

Spending Time with Jesus

Waking up thanking Him for given you another day.
Praying on your knees for being the head of your life.
Talking to Him as you brush your teeth.
When you are taking care of your functions.
Being able to wake the children for school or Church.
When you are doing your children's hair during the week.
When doing your household chores.
Writing many wonderful poems that He gives.
Reading the Word and studying.
Every time that I eat or drink something.
Meditating in a quiet room with Him.
Playing games with the children.
When teaching them about the Bible.
On the move telling others about Jesus.
Riding my bicycle somewhere the Lord gives.
Letting my light shine to the fullest it can.
Smiling no matter what something seems like.
Minding my own business and following the Lord.
Listening to Him to tell you what He wants you to do or go.

Marriage

A union between two people of the Lord.
Between a man and a woman.
A vow that to people of the opposite sex become one.
Can be done by many people who love each other.
Can be out together by God.
Can be incredible with a special connection.
Should be prayed for before joined together.
Has true meaning of love for each other.
Happiness beyond control.
Goes with the Spiritual praises of blessings.
A commitment between Christians.
Not a commitment between an unsaved and a saved person.
Does get planned and agreed to by some people.
Means different things between two people.
An experience that cannot typically be explained.
Takes place in many people lives at least once.
Growth between two people God brought together.
Someone you may have been rude to at some point.
May be what everybody wants a piece of in their life.

Lessons I Have Learned

Having people staying in my home.
Lending people money.
My personnel stuff stolen.
Being around the wrong kinds of people
Listening at people gossip about me downstairs
Having a bunch of non-Christian friends
People using my bedroom for all kinds of mess.
My money being stolen.
Being cheated on right in front of me
People in the closet doing dirt.
Lies that people tell to get what they want.
People who are backstabber's.
People who always want to look in and cannot see.
Being accused of doing things that were not true.
Almost being traded off for the wrong thing.
People trying to use me for there personal gain.
People who I have trusted I should not have.
Getting set up by different people to get jumped on.
To get hit on by people I lived with.
To be told I was hated from birth.

When Things Happen

When people are untrue, love them
Whenever someone comes against you, love them
Where there is no hope, trust in Jesus
When bills are pilled up, trust in Jesus
When people want to mistreat you, love them
When children curse at you, love them
When there is hate towards another, love them
When times are going good, trust in Jesus
When things are going your way, trust in Jesus
When the unexpected arise, trust in Jesus
Where children are dying all the time, trust in Jesus
When your family does not claim you, love them
When you can not see your way threw, trust in Jesus
When things seem to get broken, trust in Jesus
When you need help for something, trust in Jesus
When people try to steal your joy, trust in Jesus
Where there is no understanding, trust in Jesus
When things come on after another, trust in Jesus
When helping people, love them
When going out your way for another, love them
Whenever doing what the Lord wants, trust in Jesus

www.ingramcontent.com/pod-product-compliance
Lightning Source LLC
Chambersburg PA
CBHW032012080426
42735CB00007B/579